Itty Bitty
BUDDHA

T0364072

Running Press
Hachette Book Group
1290 Avenue of the Americas, New York, NY 10104
www.runningpress.com
@Running_Press

First Edition: August 2002

Published by Running Press, an imprint of Perseus Books, LLC, a subsidiary of Hachette Book Group, Inc.

The Hachette Speakers Bureau provides a wide range of authors for speaking events. To find out more, go to www.hachettespeakersbureau.com or call (866) 376-6591.

The publisher is not responsible for websites (or their content) that are not owned by the publisher.

ISBN: 978-0-7624-5940-7

About This Kit

"Buddhism does not have the answer to your question . . . You do. Only you do. The answer and the question are one and the same thing. Zen is a process, not an answering machine."

—JOHN DAIDO LOORI
in *The Heart of Being: Moral and Ethical Teachings of Zen Buddhism*

With that quote, John Daido Loori, abbot of the Zen Mountain Monastery in Mount Tremper, New York, deftly nails it. Buddhism, like any solid spiritual path, is a vehicle to enlightenment. But it is just a vehicle. It is up to you to observe the practices that will bring you the bounty the Buddha wanted for all sentient beings: the cessation of all suffering.

To reach that state of being where suffering ceases, where

you transcend the dualities of ordinary existence—pleasure and pain, heat and cold, ecstasy and misery, light and dark—is to enter into a state of blessedness so profound that every second is wondrous, life-affirming, thrilling.

This, in fact, is our natural state, but it has become covered over by conditioning and the habits of the mind. The point of Buddhism is to penetrate the coverings so you can once again live from the radiance that is at the core of your being. That is why, in Zen Buddhism, it is spoken that nirvana already exists within each and every individual. It is not something to be attained, but something to allow to unfold, just as a flower naturally unfolds. Just as the potential for a flower exists in the seed, so does the potential for enlightenment exist in every human being. Spiritual practice helps the innate Buddha nature come into its full flowering.

This kit can help you in your practice by providing you with an introduction to the teachings.

The Noble Eightfold Path

Buddha believed that the quality of "non-attachment" could be developed by subscribing to an eight-step path of practical realization. The Eightfold Path is a regimen of attitudes and actions that will eventually lead to the cessation of craving. According to Buddhist teaching, it is a systematic process that leads one to true freedom. It takes the "middle path" between extreme indulgence and radical asceticism. The individual facets of The Eightfold Path are:

RIGHT UNDERSTANDING:

Nurturing a sense of right understanding, in its simplest form, means viewing the world as it presents itself to the eye, without imposing preconceived notions.

Buddhism challenges its students to experience everything with a clear, objective mind. Thus they are to overcome the temptation to categorize things too quickly, so they may keep their perceptions neutral and view events—and people—as they actually are.

RIGHT MINDEDNESS:

Right mindedness, or right "thinking" refers to one's personal attitude. Students of Buddhism are

asked to work at eliminating pre-
conceptions, which directly influence their internal reactions to
life events.

RIGHT SPEECH:

Students of Buddhism are encour-
aged to reflect on the power of
their words and the effect they
have upon others. They are taught
to listen with awareness as they
speak, mindful of the weight their
words carry.

RIGHT ACTION:

Just as words have power, so do actions. The tenet of Right Action asks students to be aware that constructive actions have constructive effects, which return positively to the individual who initiated them. Destructive or hostile actions, similarly, initiate a chain of negative events. Students of Buddhism learn to reflect before they act, and to refrain from any actions that may harm others, and ultimately, themselves.

RIGHT LIVELIHOOD:
Buddhism teaches its students to choose work in keeping with their nature. This requires self-aware-ness and an awareness of the impact of the work on society.

That might mean, for instance, that a Buddhist practitioner chooses not to work in a plant that makes weapons. Yet what is not appropriate for one individual might be entirely appropriate for another.

RIGHT EFFORT:

Buddhist teachers exhort their students to be diligent in doing the practices that will awaken them to their innate enlightenment. Students are instructed to keep moving forward in their realization of their true nature. They are also warned to avoid laziness and indulgence, which will slow their progress. According to the teachings, right effort must be nourished with constant efforts that propel the student ever forward on the pathless path of Buddhism.

RIGHT ATTENTIVENESS:

Buddhist teachers consider an aptitude for critical thinking essential in the quest for freedom, because it allows students to recognize and acknowledge the confusion within. They consider the capacity for self-awareness valuable because it can be used to discern each and every influence that might pull a student off the spiritual path. Once a student learns to discern negative influences, she is then instructed to distance herself from them until she is able to remove herself from their sway entirely. Right attentiveness helps students of Buddhism to free themselves from cravings and the self-destructive impulses that craving generate.

RIGHT CONCENTRATION:

Concentration, in this sense, is the calm but intense focus that students of Buddhism apply in spiritual practice so they may penetrate through illusion to pure awareness. When right concentration is fully applied, it allows practitioners to enter into a state of being where there is no separation between the Buddhist meditator, the act of meditation, and object of meditation. The practice of right concentration gradually allows the Buddhist practitioner to achieve deeper and deeper focus, which is necessary to penetrate through illusions to the Ultimate Reality.

Buddhist Meditation

The teachings of Buddhism date back to Siddhatha Gautama, who was born in 563 BCE to King Suddhodana and his wife, Maya, in the Ganges valley between Nepal and Benares. Gautama is more commonly known today as Buddha (the enlightened one). Shortly after Buddha's death in 483 BCE, his followers dispersed into many diverse sects. Buddhism currently has some 500,000,000 adherents, largely in Asia, but its popularity in the West has been accelerating since the 1950s.

Just like there are many, many different forms of Christianity today, one can find many variations of Buddhism in the world.

These tend to follow along two lines: insight practices, such as Vipassana, or shamatha, which translates to "calm abiding." Jack Kornfield, a well-respected teacher of insight-style meditation, describes it as a systematic training that awakens body, heart, and mind. Shamatha-style practices are said to lead students to an intuitive understanding of the connection between themselves and every created thing.

Here in the United States, Vipassana is a popular variation, as is Zen Buddhism.

To experience Zen-style meditation, sit in a meditation pose. You can sit cross-legged on a pillow, on a meditation bench (which is low to the ground), or upright in a chair. Let your gaze focus softly on the ground in front of you. Bring your hands to your navel. Hold them in such a way that the fingers of one hand are resting in the palm of the other. Let your thumbnails just touch. Make sure your thumbnails remain that way.

The point of this is to keep you alert through the meditation so your mind is less likely to wander.

Then breathe in and mentally count "1." On the out-breath, mentally count "2." Continue in this way, counting "3" on the in-breath and "4" on the out-breath, etc., until you reach "10." Then begin the count again at "1." If you remain mindful, you will gradually unite breath and mind. If you let your mind wander, you may find yourself counting to 350 before you remember to stop at "10." That's okay, don't judge yourself. This technique can help you master your mind, which puts you in control, instead of at its mercy.

If you would like to try a basic insight meditation, sit in a meditation pose.

Let yourself relax and become aware of your breath. Notice how your body expands when you inhale and how your body contracts as you exhale.

Notice whether your breath is smooth and slow, or jagged, or if you are out-of-breath. Consider how the breath you are taking in is stimulating and energizing your cells.

As you observe your breath, notice the spaces between the in-flow and the out-flow. Consider how all of life rises and falls, in impermanence, like the breath.

(Pause and reflect.)

Keeping your awareness on your breath, let your mind become quiet. Realize that the very practice of focusing just on the breath quiets the mind, helping it settle down.

As your mind begins to quiet, allow your attention to sweep through your body, noticing the sensations that arise. Notice where there is tension, and tightness. Bring your attention to these areas. Use your awareness to penetrate the center of these areas of discomfort, and to "hold the edges" of the discomfort with loving attentiveness. Observe how your loving attention, which you will continue to hold on these areas for a few moments, changes the sensations. Perhaps the tension dissolves, or insight arises from the soft focus of your attention.

When it feels appropriate, do another body scan. Notice where there is openness and ease. Allow your mind to dwell there for a few moments. Then allow yourself to hold your entire body in awareness. Notice the sensations, the movement within, the life permeating it. Breathe in and out with awareness, opening to the life within.

If you would like to try a mantra-style meditation that is popular among adherents of Tibetan Buddhism, seat yourself comfortably in a meditation posture and chant:

Om-mani-padme hum. That translates roughly to the "jewel in the lotus," a symbol of the eternal self. The six syllables are said to be associated with the six realms of existence. Keep repeating the mantra over and over, out loud, and then silently if you like, trying to keep your entire focus on the mantra. If your mind wanders—which it probably will, at least in the beginning—bring your awareness back. Keep your focus on the mantra so pure that you feel yourself begin to merge with the sounds.

The Eightfold Path, as outlined above, requires commitment to a meditation practice, plus careful, mindful choices about one's intentions, speech, actions, choice of work, application of effort, etc. Again, it points the way but it does not guarantee the result. That's up to you and the depth of your practice. As Zen Abbott John Daido Loori points out in *The*

Heart of Being: Moral and Ethical Teachings of Zen Buddhism:

"The Buddha Way is not about belief systems. It is about empowering yourself, realizing yourself, finding the answer in yourself. Your own direct experience of realization, and then actualization of that realization in the world . . . It has to flow out of your heart."

This book has been bound using
handcraft methods and Smyth-sewn
to ensure durability.

The package, book cover and interior
were designed by Susan Van Horn.

The text was written by Nicola Dixon
and edited by Deborah Grandinetti.

The text was set in BPreplay and
XXII Awesome Script.

Package border art ©Thinkstock/Chunhai Cao.
Radial graphic ©Thinkstock/Christophe Boisson.
Buddha illustration by Susan Van Horn.